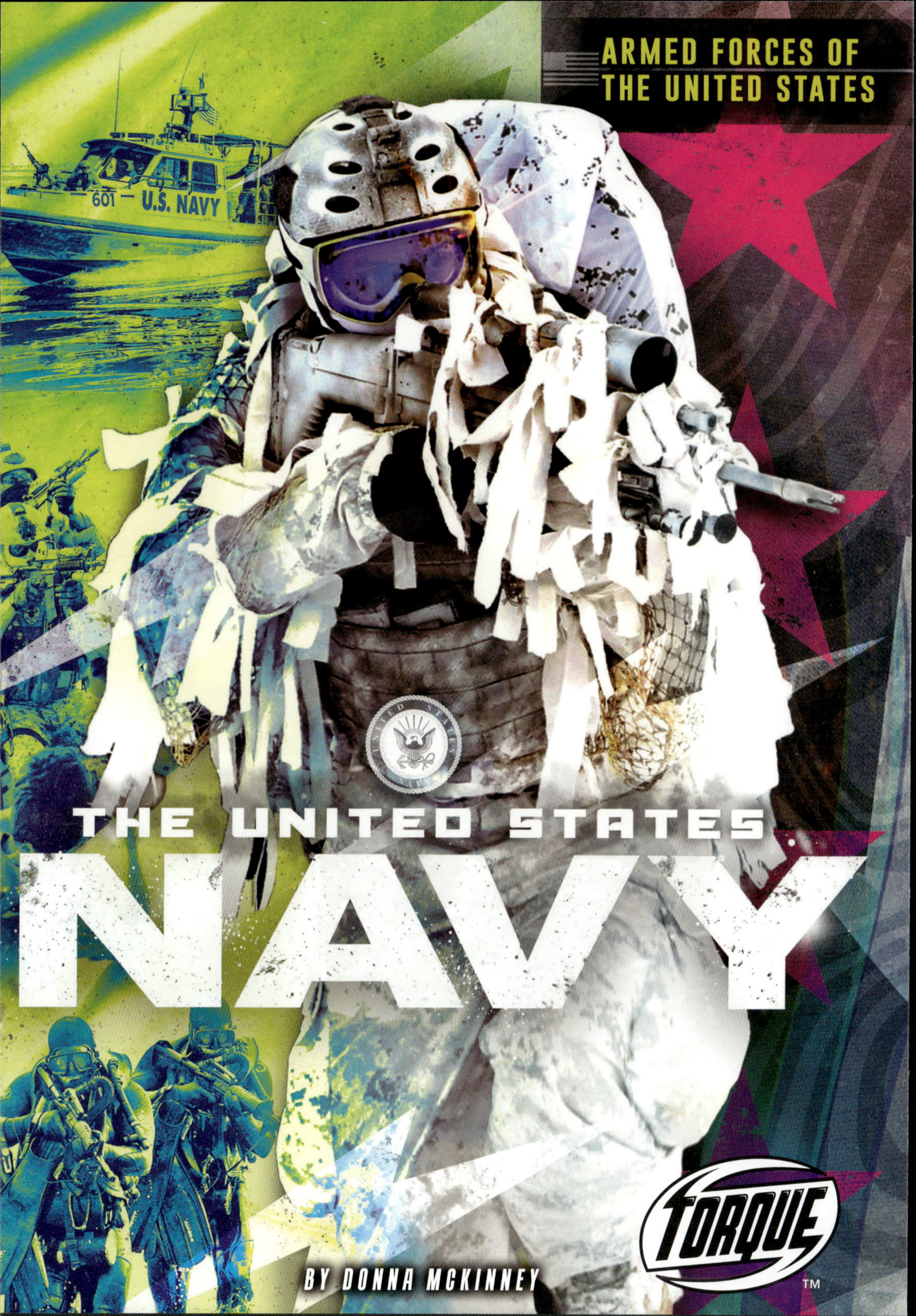

ARMED FORCES OF THE UNITED STATES

THE UNITED STATES NAVY

BY DONNA MCKINNEY

TORQUE™

BELLWETHER MEDIA • MINNEAPOLIS, MN

TORQUE™

Torque brims with excitement perfect for thrill-seekers of all kinds. Discover daring survival skills, explore uncharted worlds, and marvel at mighty engines and extreme sports. In *Torque* books, anything can happen. Are you ready?

This edition first published in 2025 by Bellwether Media, Inc.

Library of Congress Cataloging-in-Publication Data

Names: McKinney, Donna B. (Donna Bowen), author.
Title: The United States Navy / by Donna McKinney.
Description: Minneapolis, MN : Bellwether Media, Inc., 2025. | Series: Armed forces of the United States | Includes bibliographical references and index. | Audience: Ages 7-12 | Audience: Grades 4-6 |
Summary: "Engaging images accompany information about the United States Navy. The combination of high-interest subject matter and light text is intended for students in grades 3 through 7"–Provided by publisher.
Identifiers: LCCN 2024016005 (print) | LCCN 2024016006 (ebook) | ISBN 9798893040142 (library binding) | ISBN 9781644879467 (ebook)
Subjects: LCSH: United States. Navy–Juvenile literature.
Classification: LCC VA58.4 .M3777 2025 (print) | LCC VA58.4 (ebook) | DDC 359.00973–dc23/eng/20240410
LC record available at https://lccn.loc.gov/2024016005
LC ebook record available at https://lccn.loc.gov/2024016006

Editor: Rebecca Sabelko Designer: Jeffrey Kollock

Printed in the United States of America, North Mankato, MN.

TABLE OF CONTENTS

FLOATING HOSPITALS

USNS COMFORT

USNS MERCY

It is spring 2020. Many people are sick with the **Covid-19 virus**. Hospitals everywhere have run out of room for patients. The United States Navy sends hospital ships to help. USNS *Mercy* travels to Los Angeles. USNS *Comfort* travels to New York City.

Both ships have 1,000 beds for patients. They have 12 operating rooms. The Navy cares for patients in those cities.

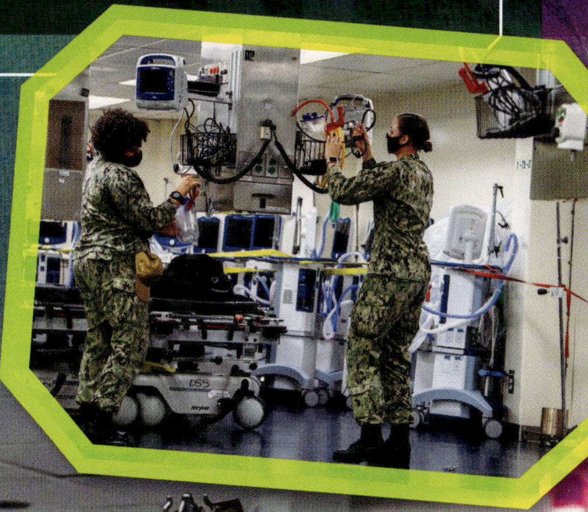

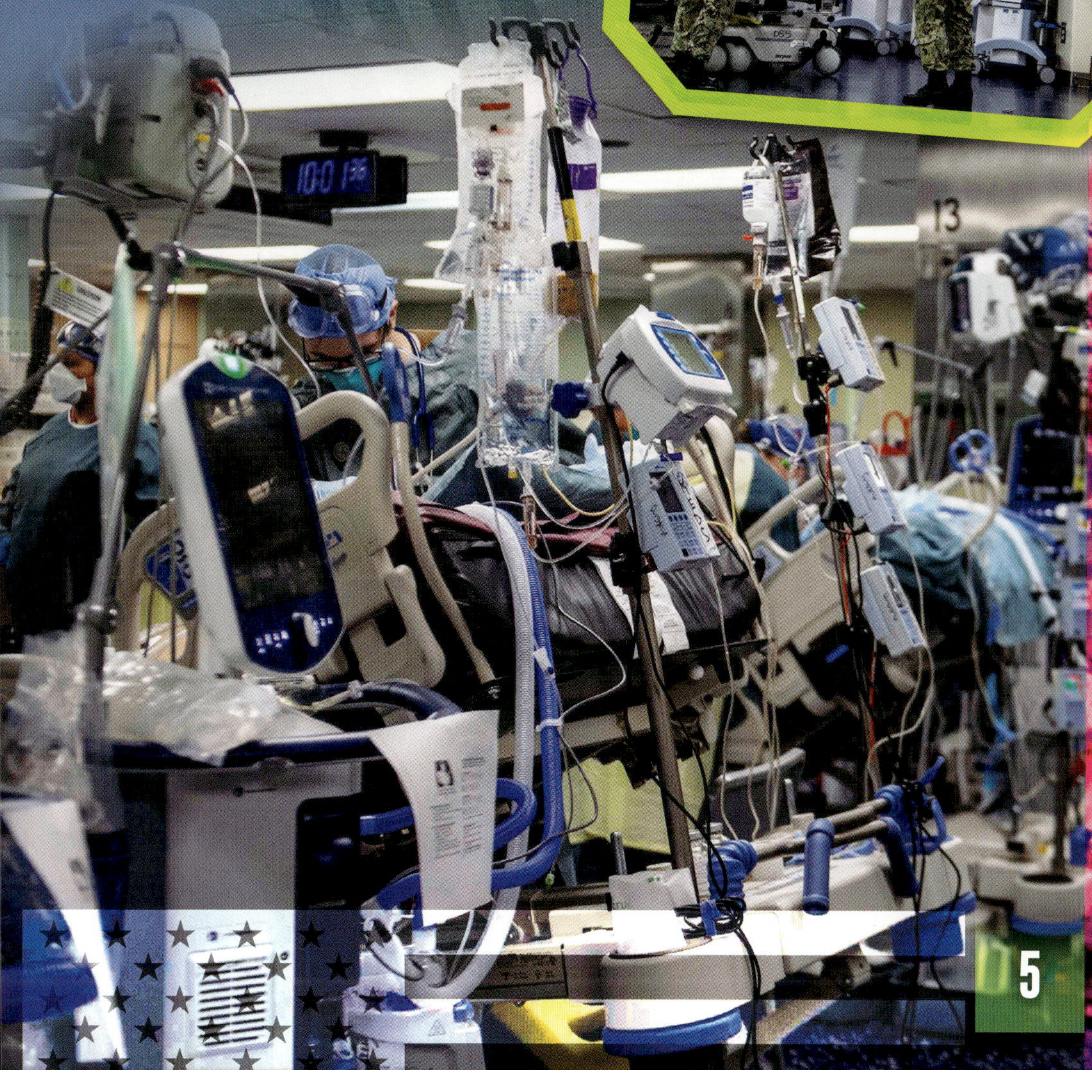

DEFENDING THE SEAS

The Navy carries out U.S. military **missions** at sea. They patrol waters around the world. People who serve are called Sailors. Sailors work on ships and **submarines**, or subs. They also use aircraft to conduct missions.

The **Pentagon** is the Navy **headquarters**. Navy **bases** are in the U.S. and overseas. Most Sailors spend time living aboard ships or subs. These **vessels** travel around the world.

SAILORS ON A SUB

NAVAL ACADEMY

The Naval Academy is in Annapolis, Maryland. Students become Naval or Marine Corps officers when they finish school.

NAVY BASE IN HAWAII

PENTAGON

Navy vessels travel where U.S. Army land forces cannot go. These vessels are armed with powerful weapons. Ships also carry aircraft to launch air attacks against enemies. Their presence sometimes stops fights from starting.

In peacetime, Sailors help when **natural disasters** happen. They rescue people at sea. They keep waters safe from crime.

NAVY BASES

NAVY SHIPS, SUBS, AND AIRCRAFT

The Navy's biggest warships are aircraft **carriers**. They are about the length of three football fields! Aircraft take off from the ships' decks. Carriers are also armed with different kinds of **missiles**.

LITTORAL COMBAT SHIP

NUMBER IN USE AS OF 2023 | 25

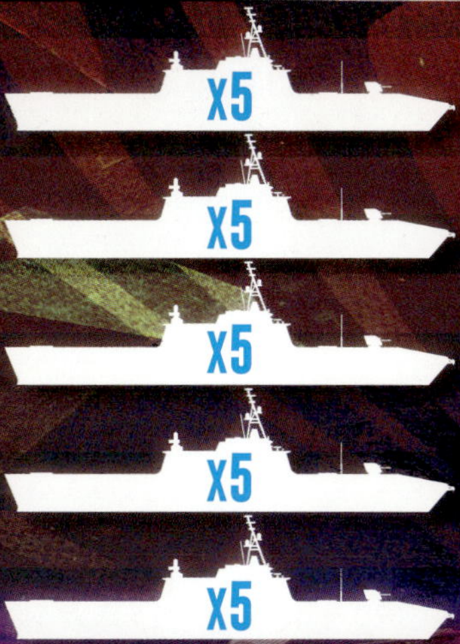

WHAT IS IT? A FAST WARSHIP MADE FOR KEEPING U.S. WATERS NEAR THE SHORES SAFE

FIRST USED 2002

SUPER HORNET FIGHTER JET

The newest carriers hold 90 aircraft. They carry Super Hornet fighters and Advanced Hawkeyes. They also carry helicopters and **drones**.

Sailors on subs live and work underwater. Subs rise to the surface when Sailors need supplies. Drones, airplanes, or helicopters drop supplies to subs.

SAILORS INSIDE A SUB

Subs are built to hide from enemies. Attack subs can fire weapons at enemy subs and ships. They also fire Tomahawk missiles at land targets. Some subs are armed with powerful **nuclear weapons**.

MISSIONS

The army of Iraq invaded Kuwait in 1990. This started the Persian Gulf War. Many countries fought against Iraq. U.S. Navy ships quickly sailed to the Persian Gulf to fight.

More than 240 Navy ships were in the area. They brought gear that soldiers needed to fight land battles. Navy carriers delivered aircraft that carried out air strikes in Iraq.

NAVY TEAM

The Marine Corps is part of the U.S. Navy. The Coast Guard becomes part of the Navy during wartime.

SEPTEMBER 11, 2001, ATTACK

SAILORS IN SPACE

Navy astronaut Alan Shepard was the first American in space. Navy astronaut Neil Armstrong was the first person to stand on the Moon.

OSAMA BIN LADEN

Terrorist leader Osama bin Laden led the September 11, 2001, terrorist attacks. The U.S. military spent years trying to find him. They carried out a special mission called Operation Neptune Spear.

Army pilots flew Navy **SEALs** to bin Laden's hideout in Pakistan on May 1, 2011. The SEALs landed at night. They used night-vision goggles to find him.

ACTOR PORTRAYAL OF OPERATION NEPTUNE SPEAR

THE NATIONAL SECURITY TEAM WATCHING OPERATION NEPTUNE SPEAR

Some Navy missions help people in need. Hurricane Katrina struck the U.S. Gulf Coast in 2005. The Navy sent aircraft, warships, and 10,000 Sailors. Sailors searched for missing people. They treated injuries. They brought supplies.

HURRICANE KATRINA RESCUE MISSION

The Navy sails ships on the world's oceans. Its subs move through waters unseen. Its aircraft protect the skies. The Navy works to keep the country safe.

MISSION

OPERATION TOMODACHI (OPERATION FRIEND)

DATE MARCH 2011

PURPOSE

A NAVY SUPPORT MISSION FOLLOWING AN EARTHQUAKE IN JAPAN

RESULTS

THE NAVY SENT 24 SHIPS, 190 AIRCRAFT, AND OVER 24,000 SAILORS TO HELP JAPAN RECOVER

NAVY PROFILE

MEMBERS TO REMEMBER

ENSIGN JESSE BROWN
The first Black Naval aviator

REAR ADMIRAL GRACE HOPPER
A Naval officer and computer pioneer

ADMIRAL HYMAN RICKOVER
"Father of the nuclear Navy"

MISSIONS

THE INVASION OF NORMANDY
1944

VIETNAM WAR
1950 to 1975

OPERATION IRAQI FREEDOM
2003

EMBLEM

LOGO

MOTTO "Not self, but country"

YEAR ESTABLISHED 1775

NUMBER OF MEMBERS

active duty in 2023 more than 331,000

RANKS

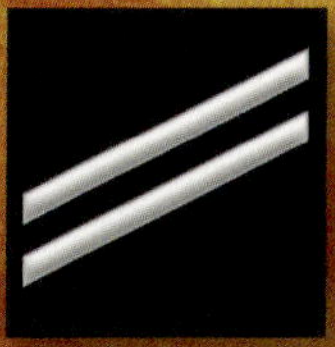

Seaman Apprentice

Admiral

GLOSSARY

bases—places where armed forces train and work

carriers—warships that are airbases for aircraft to land on and take off from at sea

Covid-19 virus—an illness that started in December 2019 that led to millions of deaths and shutdowns around the world

drones—aircraft that are flown by a remote control or by computers

headquarters—the main office of an organization

missiles—weapons that travel in the air and explode when they hit targets

missions—jobs that Navy headquarters assigns to Sailors

natural disasters—natural events, such as floods, earthquakes, or hurricanes, that cause damage

nuclear weapons—bombs that use nuclear power to create powerful explosions

Pentagon—a building in Arlington, Virginia, that is headquarters for the U.S. military

SEALs—Sea, Air, and Land teams; Navy SEALs are forces that carry out the most dangerous missions.

submarines—vessels that are used underwater

terrorist—related to a person who uses fear to control others

vessels—ships and submarines

TO LEARN MORE

AT THE LIBRARY

Adamson, Thomas K. *Hurricane Katrina.* Minneapolis, Minn.: Bellwether Media, 2022.

McKinney, Donna. *F/A-18 E/F Super Hornet.* Minneapolis, Minn.: Bellwether Media, 2024.

Monroe, Alex. *The Vietnam War.* Minneapolis, Minn.: Bellwether Media, 2024.

ON THE WEB

FACTSURFER

Factsurfer.com gives you a safe, fun way to find more information.

1. Go to www.factsurfer.com
2. Enter "The United States Navy" into the search box and click 🔍.
3. Select your book cover to see a list of related content.

INDEX

The images in this book are reproduced through the courtesy of: DVIDS, front cover, pp. 4, 5 (main, inset), 7 (top, fun fact, middle), 8, 10, 11 (main, Littoral Combat Ship), 12 (main, inset), 13 (inset), 19 (left, right), 23; AlejandroCarnicero, p. 3; Navy Medicine/ Wikipedia Commons, p. 4 (inset); Vytautas Kielaitis, p. 6; Jeremy Christensen, p. 7 (bottom); US Navy/ Wikipedia Commons, pp. 8 (inset), 9 (Naval Base Kitsap, Naval Station Norfolk, Naval Air Station Jacksonville, Naval Base San Diego, Joint Base Pearl Harbor-Hickam), 13, 18 (inset), 20 (Brown, Hopper, Rickover, The Invasion of Normandy, Operation Iraqi Freedom), 21 (emblem, logo, Seaman Apprentice, Admiral); R. J. Worsley/ Wikipedia Commons, p. 14; US Navy/ National Museum of the US Navy, p. 15 (top); DOD Photo/ Alamy, p. 15 (middle); SuperStock/ Alamy, p. 15 (bottom); rds323/ Wikipedia Commons, p. 16; Hamid Mir/ Wikipedia Commons, p. 16 (inset); NASA/ Wikipedia Commons, p. 16 (fun fact); Photo 12/ Alamy, p. 17 (top); Pete Souza/ Wikipedia Commons, p. 17 (bottom); Abaca Press/ Alamy, p. 18; US Navy/ National Archives, p. 20 (Vietnam War).